WACO-M

WACO TX 76701

THIS BEAUTY

IS A

BEAST

ELAINE DAVIS

LifeRich PUBLISHING

LifeRich Publishing is a registered trademark of The Reader's Digest Association, Inc.

LifeRich Publishing books may be ordered through booksellers or by contacting:

LifeRich Publishing
1663 Liberty Drive
Bloomington, IN 47403
www.liferichpublishing.com
1 (888) 238-8637

ISBN: 978-1-4897-2994-1 (sc)
ISBN: 978-1-4897-3008-4 (e)

Print information available on the last page.

LifeRich Publishing rev. date: 07/21/2020

This book is dedicated to anyone who has ever been told "you cannot do it". No matter how hard it gets, never let anything or anyone stop you from becoming what you are destined to be. Life is only what you make it, so be sure to make the best of it. Never let the negative energy in your life drain your positive energy, only let it charge you into becoming a better you. This book will show you how a rose in the concrete broke through and blossomed. I am a product of my environment, but I am here to show you what my environment has to offer. You cannot have the mindset that where you came from can stop you from achieving your goals. All you have to do is set your mind on reaching them. Only you know your capabilities. You just have to believe in yourself, speak positive words, and watch yourself prosper. I am living proof. This is just the beginning of greatness.

ACKNOWLEDGMENTS

I would like to thank God, who gave me the ability to do the great things I am doing in life. I would also like to thank my amazing husband who has helped me see the greatness that I held within. He has always been by my side, no matter what and I love him with everything in me. I also would like to thank Eryka Parker, my editor with Lyrical Innovations LLC, for assisting me with this project. She did an amazing job helping me and I really appreciate her. She knew exactly what I wanted to say and how I wanted to say it and I definitely recommend her to anyone. I would also like to thank all my family and friends for your continued support and love.

SECTION ONE

THE EYES OF A CHILD

My birth certificate lists my mother name while the field for my father's name is blank. My earliest memory was at three years old. While in preschool, I remember watching other kids being picked up and dropped off by their fathers. I would always wonder who my father was. I was born and raised in Cleveland, Ohio and over the course of my childhood, I thought three different guys were my father. I couldn't understand why I didn't know who he was or why he didn't want me. The pain of not having a father was very impactful on my life. Why would he bring a child into the world and not take care of it? I remember my guardian meeting a guy, who is now my stepfather, and when I was little, I called him by his name. But as I got older, I began calling him "Dad". Any man can be a father, but it takes a real man to be a Dad. Life was not easy while I was growing up. I lived in a duplex with three bedrooms and an attic. There were three separate families living in one house and our family consisted of my mother, myself, and my three siblings. The other families consisted of my aunt and her two children, my uncle and his three children, and my grandmother. There was a total of thirteen of us living under one roof, and I don't know how we did it, but we managed.

All of the kids in the house attended the same school. Due to the size of our family and our close ages, everyone knew who the Davis family was. We always walked to and from school together in a big group, holding hands. I miss the good old days with my siblings and cousins. It felt like we were all sisters and brothers because we all stayed in the same household. But as we got older, we began outgrowing the space and the adults were no longer able to see eye to eye.

I remember seeing my grandmother slap my mother in the face because she thought she had stolen her money. My mother was at work at the time it happened, but my grandmother kicked my mother and her kids out without us having a place to go. We moved in with my godmother down the street until we were able to find another place to live. We moved in with my mother's male friend, Rob. He lived in a one-bedroom apartment in the projects. I was about six years old at the time and had to sleep with my brothers, John and Lamar, and my older sister, Sasha on the living room floor or couch.

As time went on, things began looking better for us. I finally had a father figure in my life, and we all lived together in one place. After a while, I started to notice Rob leaving the house for days at a time, I didn't understand what was going on at that time. But I knew something wasn't right. After a while, my mother got pregnant and had my little brother, Jacob, her fifth child. He was so handsome and I was happy to have another brother. Rob and my mother would always have disagreements that turned physical at times, they would always make up afterward, but I began to dislike him for what he was doing to her. I believe we all did.

Because we lived in the projects, we couldn't go outside. So, when we started to run around indoors, playing and doing things that kids do, Rob would whoop us. I couldn't help feeling like hope was fading fast. It was boring staying inside the house all the time because we didn't have much to do. I felt unloved and the constant arguing amongst ourselves was a result of taking the anger our situation caused out on each other.

Sasha and I were especially at odds with one another. When I was eight years old, we moved out of the projects and into a three-bedroom unit in a two-family house, which felt more like home. The set of boys and girls each shared rooms and we were excited to have our own beds. Rob's leaving in and out of the house continued and became more frequent. Eventually, my mother began leaving the older children in charge, stating she would "be right back". My mother got pregnant with

2

my little sister, Autumn, and delivered her prematurely. She weighed only two pounds. My mother almost died giving birth to her and had to have two blood transfusions. I don't know what would have happened to us if my mother had passed away. We would have probably all been split up and sent to foster homes. We were staying with Rob's mother who told us she was not our grandmother and to call her by her name. She would say mean things to us like, "your parents are going to die". I used to think something was really wrong with her and couldn't wait to get back home.

When my mother got home from the hospital, we were elated to see her. She hugged and kissed us and I loved every moment of it. Rob was still in and out of the house and rarely stayed there with us. A month later, Autumn finally came home from the hospital. She was so beautiful and tiny; I was scared to hold her. Soon after, my mother began leaving us home alone again. My little sister needed me, so I always took care of her. I would look my baby sister in the eyes and tell her "I will always be here". She would smile at me and that made me happy. My older sister used to stay with my godmother. I preferred it when she was gone because she and I didn't get along well. When I was in the fifth grade, my godmother died in a house fire along with my god brother and god sister. On top of that, my fifth-grade teacher also passed away. I felt like I couldn't take the stress of having so much on my plate at a young age anymore. In the middle of the school year, I began to think that something may have been wrong with me. I would have to take tests in a private room because I was unable to focus while around others. My main concern was going home and making sure my younger siblings were okay.

I still felt unloved by my mother, but I felt close to my younger siblings. I let them know that I would always be there for them no matter what. When I reached my sixth-grade year, I was placed in special education classes. I was bullied at home and school by my own sister who called me names like stupid, retarded, dummy, and ugly. One day, Sasha was walking down the hallway at school with a boy and he said, "there's your sister". She looked right at me, laughed, and said, "that's not my sister". Hearing her deny me like that hurt me so bad.

I got sick of her demeaning me and would confront her about it. We would always fight and could never see eye to eye. I'd always felt like my mother showed favoritism to her. She would buy Sasha a pair of Lebron James tennis shoes and I would get a pair from Payless. I was not materialistic so I didn't get upset about it, but I began to wonder why I couldn't get the same shoes my sister had. My mother would also buy my school clothes baggy while my sister's clothes fit perfectly. I was bullied because of my baggy pants and people used to say I had a diaper on. It hurt my feelings so much, but I just buried it with the rest of my pain. When we finally moved into a single-family house, I got my own bedroom and space apart from my sister was good for me. It allowed me to deal with the way she was treating me. But Rob was still in and out of the house and he had begun selling things from our house to feed his addiction. That was when I realized he was on drugs and, shortly after, he began using drugs in the house in front of us. The smell was distinct and strong, and I'll never forget it. I watched him use a piece of burnt glass to smoke his drugs and I later learned it was called a crack pipe. Each time he would leave it lying around, I would toss them in the trash to keep Jacob and Autumn from discovering them.

My life felt surreal and I began to regret not having a childhood because I always had to be strong for my little siblings. They relied on me to be the parent while both parents were abusing alcohol and drugs. I felt their actions were selfish and forced me into an adult role in order to provide stability in my siblings' lives. My pent-up anger began to come out more in various ways. I would shut my bedroom door and destroy everything inside, punching my walls, pulling my hair, and screaming at the top of my lungs. Afterward, I would kneel and pray, hoping that God could hear me. I would cry so long and hard that my eyes would be swollen shut. I felt misunderstood and like I had no one to discuss my feelings with. When I would go into the bathroom to pull myself together after my outbursts, I would look in the mirror and all I saw was my ugly face. I would hear dumb, retarded, and stupid girl in the voice of my only big sister, my flesh and blood. In those moments, I wanted to take my own life to ease the pain. But then I would hear my little sister crying, which made me realize that they needed me. I knew

I couldn't leave my siblings because they would have no one to look out for them. They needed me to be strong for them, so I took a deep breath, bottled up my pain, and went to check on her. When she saw me, she began to smile and I would smile back at her, telling her that I loved her and kissing her on the forehead. I told her that everything would be okay, and some ways I was also telling myself.

Christmas was approaching and my mother didn't have much money saved up for our gifts. But when she was sober, she always made a way out of no way for us. She managed to get some presents for us that year. But when I came downstairs one day, the Grinch was trying to take everything he could get his hands on in order to feed his addiction. I asked Rob, "Why are you doing this to us?"

He smiled, blinking his eyes rapidly, clutching the bag, and asked, "Doing what?"

I turned around to go investigate whether it was the Christmas gifts for me and my siblings in his bag. Thank God it wasn't. I decided to wrap our gifts in newspaper because we couldn't afford Christmas wrapping paper. I hid our gifts under my bed and each night, I would sleep on the floor in front of my bed to make sure he couldn't get to them.

Christmas was my favorite holiday because I loved to put up the tree with my younger siblings and see the smiles on their faces when it lit up. Their joy was priceless on Christmas day when they wake up to see their presents under the tree. Seeing them that way gave me so much hope. It was great to have one day of family togetherness without the interference of drugs or alcohol. I would always tell myself that if my parents failed to get themselves together, I would figure out a way to get custody of them once I was old enough. It was my biggest fear that we would be separated, so I would often lie at school when they would have questions about my home life due to my emotional issues. I made it a point not to discuss anything that would allude to the fact that our home life wasn't ideal. I stepped up when it came to my younger siblings' needs so there would be no suspicion of issues in their home life either.

I begin to lose track of important tasks that I needed to get done for school. I wasn't able to comprehend any of my subjects in school with the exception of art, physical education, and music class. I enjoyed running around and playing games with the other kids in gym class and it was the only time I felt like a kid. Everyone was smiling, laughing, and enjoying themselves and it felt good to just be free. I was actually disappointed when the school day ended because I had to return to reality. I remember going to my godmother's house before she passed away and I didn't like it very much. She treated my older sister better than me, just as my mother did. As a result, I found myself hanging out in my godbrother's room for the majority of the time I spent there. He was fun to be around; we would laugh and have a great time passing time together. But one day, he began touching me inappropriately and having me do things a child should not be doing. I never told anyone about what he'd done because I didn't think anyone would believe me. Besides, he told me he would hurt me if I ever said anything to anyone about it. All I could think about was my little brothers and sister and I blinded myself from my own pain. I knew I had to be strong for them. From that point on, I couldn't stand going over there anymore and avoided it whenever I could.

When I started the seventh grade, Rob stopped doing drugs in the house. He made the decision to get help for his addiction and was gone for a long time. We visited him in rehab on Sundays and would have dinner with him. God had answered my prayers because I'd longed for days like that for years. A year later, Rob was still drug-free, and no one could tell me that God wasn't real. My mother had also cut back on drinking and we started doing more things together as a family. It wasn't all perfect, though. Sasha, Lamar, and John did not care for Rob. They would call him by his first name and Sasha was often disrespectful to him and my mother. They used to let her get away with a lot and it only worsened when she got older.

Meanwhile, my parents' increasing presence at home allowed me to finally start living my own life. At fourteen years old, most girls my age were into boys and makeup. I was so behind, I just wanted to play outside. I mostly played with kids younger than me, trying to catch up on my childhood. I used to love jumping on my friend's trampoline and we used to always play with Barbie dolls it was so much fun to feel like a little kid again. She was about 6 years younger than me but she nor her mother ever treated me differently because of my age. People used to tell me I was too old to be playing with her, but I never listened to them. We played all day and night until the streetlights came on. I don't think they even knew how old I was because I was short and looked young for my age.

At school, the girls in my grade would always discuss the boys they liked, and I wouldn't have anything to contribute to the conversation. I was in my own little world back then and didn't realize that when boys would mess with you, it was because they liked you. I would get into it with boys in my class all the time, particularly one boy. He would always mess with me and we always got into it. His mom would predict that we would get married one day and I would protest, saying, "No, we're not!"

One day in class, he hinted that he had something to tell me. The next thing I knew, he was kissing me. I was outdone. Before I could stop myself, I began hitting him. Although he never hit me back, I could tell he was mad. I had feelings for him but didn't know how to handle it. I'd never had a conversation with anyone about boys and how it was natural for me to feel that way toward him. I used to fight a lot of females during the eighth grade because it seemed like they would all try me. I've never been a friendly person or had many friendships because I didn't see the need for them. Fighting helped me release all of the pent-up anger I've had in me for years. People would normally leave me alone, but there were a few people that would seem to test me for no reason. They would call me names and say, "That's why you're in a slow class." Their teasing reminded me of how my sister would talk down to me and the worst would come out of me. People would call me the Hulk because when I got to the point where the ugliness came out of me, there was no stopping me. I never understood why people bullied others to that point.

In the eighth grade, I met my real father. Yes, I said my real father – the man that did not sign my birth certificate, the man that never showed his face and left me guessing about his identity up until that point in my life. I honestly believed he didn't exist. One day, a lady pulled up in front of our house and asked me if my name was Elaine. My first instinct was to get smart with her because I figured she was coming to start some mess with me. I didn't know if she wanted to fight or if she was just looking for trouble.

Then she said, "My name is Summer, and I think y'all are my little sisters."

I was instantly excited at the thought that I had a big sister that I knew nothing about. She pulled into the driveway and my siblings and I went inside to get our mom, who welcomed her into the house. As soon as my mom saw her, she said, "Yup, that's your sister."

Summer looked like us and I couldn't stop smiling because I felt like I had a second chance at developing a healthy relationship with an older sister. When she told us that there were more siblings and that I had more older sisters and an older brother, a younger sister, and younger brothers, I was ecstatic. She told me I looked a lot like my grandmother on my father's side and that I looked like my two other older sisters. I was amazed and thrilled to learn more about my siblings and the other members of my family.

Then she let us know that our father was not in any of my other siblings' lives either, with the exception of the three youngest children. When I met one of my older sisters, I saw that we did look just alike, as Summer said. She was beautiful. Her nose was large, just like mine – it was the same nose people would look at on my face and call me ugly – but when I looked at her, I told myself I was beautiful, too. When we got ready to visit my father, I didn't know what to think. I wasn't sure if I even wanted to go, but I pushed myself to take the trip because I knew I had to. I felt happiness and anger at the same time as we took the short drive to his house. My mind was everywhere – wondering how he looked, what I would say to him, and what he would say to me. Before I knew it, we pulled in front of his house and as she parked the car, I could barely lift my feet to get out of the car. My heartbeat so rapidly in my chest, it hurt. As we got out of the car and walked up to the house, I could hear my pulse thumping in my eardrums. I wiped my sweaty palms on my shirt and followed my sister into the house.

When I laid eyes on my father, I froze. He was short and dark-skinned and looked similar to me. All of the thoughts and emotions I'd just been experiencing instantly drained away from me. I couldn't move and felt like I was in a dream as I stared at him, taking every inch of him in. I was literally waiting to wake up, but the reality of the situation was slowly sinking in. He moved to hug my sister, then came over to me and hugged me. My body instantly grew cold and my words were stuck in my throat. My mind frantically searched for something to say, but there were no words. He noticed my reaction to him and immediately labeled me as "the mean one".

He attempted to explain himself, blaming my mother for keeping us away from him. One thing was for sure and two were for certain, I had a lot of common sense at that age and there was no way that anyone could convince me that a man who really wanted to see his children would allow anyone to keep him away from them. He would certainly find a way to get to us if it was important to him. Besides, I knew he was lying because my mother had gone to court to be awarded child support. He said we weren't his children so that he wouldn't have to pay But when the judge took one look at him and my sister, she put him behind bars because we look like our father. He has very strong genes.

I just stood there and let him continue to talk. The fact that he would use this opportunity to lie on my mother was disgusting. He wasn't going to own up to anything and I knew there was no way I would be able to respect him. I was ready to leave almost as soon as I'd arrived. I was ready to look past him and meet the rest of his family in order to have a healthy connection with his side of my family. The last thing I wanted to do was grow up and end up unknowingly dating one of my family members. That ended up being the first and last time I'd seen my father in good health. He passed away from prostate cancer in 2015, about eleven years after I met him. On his death bed, I told him that I forgave him, even though I hadn't yet because I didn't want him to die thinking I hated him. I resented the fact that I'd never gotten the chance to get to know him. When I got the call that he'd passed away, I went to view his body in the hospice. Several of his family members were there, but many of them did not recognize me. Once my aunt, my father's sister, informed them that I was his daughter, they immediately realized it.

As I stood there, looking at his dead body, surrounded by sobbing family members, I was void of emotion. The only tears I shed were while I was at his funeral, as I stood, staring at the casket and wondering why I'd never gotten the chance to get to know my own father. It was at that moment that I felt the pain as my heart crushed under the pressure of all of the emotions, I'd pushed down deep inside of myself. I began thinking about all of the talks I would never have with him and the male figure I would never be able to turn to for advice and guidance throughout my life. I thought of all I'd lost that I'd never had. I will always have a blank spot in my heart that can never be filled because only my real father could do that for me. I only see my father's side of the family at funerals or large family gatherings now and I still don't know some of them.

Once I started high school, I was still playing with toys. On Christmas day, there was a wrapped gift with an E on it. I opened it, thinking it was mine and was super exited because it was a Barbie doll. My mother took it out of my hands and told me I was too old to be playing with toys, and it was my little sister's doll. I was so hurt. From that point on, I turned my attention to boys. I was a little awkward and clueless when dealing with them and would often feel uncomfortable around them. When a male friend of mine told me that his friend liked me, I responded, "how does he like me when he doesn't even know me?" He encouraged me to get to know him and I let him know that his friend could come over and get to know me himself. Next thing I knew, the friend was making his way over and introducing himself as Leon. I looked up and took in his handsome smile, nice teeth, and nice shoes. I also couldn't stop staring into his beautiful brown eyes.

He asked, "Can I have your phone number so we can get to know each other?"

I agreed and rushed home to wait for his call. As soon as I got to my bedroom, he called and we stayed on the phone for hours. After a month of talking every single day, we decided to go together. I was happy, excited, and nervous to have my first boyfriend. I was only in the ninth grade so dating someone was all new to me. To top it off, he was a junior and my female classmates would gas me up, saying, "Oh my God, you have a boyfriend in the eleventh grade!" I didn't think it was a big deal and saw Leon for who he was, not how old he was. Shortly after we began dating, the popular kids began to notice me. They would speak to me all the time and even referred to us as "Bonnie and Clyde" because you'd never see one of us without the other outside of class.

After a while, Leon brought up the topic of sex, asking me if I'd ever had it before. I was hesitant to discuss it with him because I'd never talked about it with anyone before. But because I liked him so much, I admitted that I was a virgin. Next, he began telling me how beautiful I was and how much he loved me. It was the first time anyone had said those words to me and after getting used to being called ugly, his words made a huge impact on me. I fell for him even harder and we spent more time together as the weeks passed. One day, he told me his mother was going to move him back to Mississippi with his grandmother. He sounded as devastated as I'd felt. I began to cry and that was when he asked me to have sex with him. He said I would be his first and that he loved me. I couldn't see myself with anyone else, but I cried and let him know how important my body was to me. I agreed to have sex with him, despite my fears and my ignorance about what it really involved. I'd never discussed sex with my friends or family, so I didn't know what to expect. The only thing I knew about it was what I'd seen in the movies. But I felt like the amount of love I thought I had for him made me ready to take the next step with him.

In retrospect, I realize that losing my virginity to Leon was one of the worst choices I'd made. We went from talking every day to days passing by without me hearing a word from him. He went from being my sweet, devoted boyfriend to acting as though he didn't even know me. I would call and he would always be too busy to speak to me. His mother and sister would answer the phone and lie for him, telling me that he wasn't home. Once I finally got him to speak to me, he informed me that he was no longer moving. He said he loved me and apologized for acting funny toward me. Despite all of the stress he'd put me through, I still forgave him and accepted his half-apology. Over time, I noticed that the only time he wanted to be bothered with me was when we were able to have sex. Eager to spend time with him, I agreed to have frequent sex with him. He still called me beautiful, sexy, and smart and that he loved me. Although I didn't enjoy having sex, due to the assault I'd experienced at a young age, I craved the connection with Leon. I'd given him my virginity because I felt like he was deserving of the only precious thing I had left. But I was wrong.

PAIN RUNS DEEP

Soon after we reunited, he began acting distant again. Once again, he was too busy, not home, and unavailable to speak to me or spend time. I soon grew tired of him avoiding me. I asked a family friend to call him and give his sister a fake name when she answered. Sure enough, she put her on hold and Leon came right to the phone. I was angry with him for having his sister lie to me and we got into an argument that ended with me hanging up on him. I investigated his recent actions some more and learned that he had been cheating on me. To confirm when I called his house, later on, his sister called me by another name. I just hung up, fed up with the lies and drama.

He ended up calling me back hours later as if nothing ever happened. I played right along and agreed to meet up with him in the morning to talk. The next morning, I told him how much I loved him, and he told me he felt the same way. Then I asked him if he was seeing someone else and he denied it. He began kissing me and even though I hadn't believed one word he said, I allowed one thing to lead to another. A part of me was still holding on to the relationship, regardless of the information I'd discovered about his infidelity. Everything seemed fine when we got to school, but by the end of the day, I got a phone call from a friend. She told me to come downtown because she'd just seen Leon in a store buying a girl a pair of shoes. Initially, I doubted what I'd been told, mostly because I had just been with him that morning and we'd had a talk about the state of our relationship. He'd confirmed to my face that he hadn't been seeing anyone else. But I still headed downtown and made it just in time to see him and the girl together.

As soon as they walked out of the store, I asked, "So, it's like that?"

He looked straight in my face and said, "Yeah, it's like that."

I felt so enraged, betrayed, and hurt that I couldn't control myself. I punched him dead in his eye. Then I asked the girl if she wanted some of me as well.

She said, "I don't have time to fight. I'm pregnant and Leon is the father."

I felt hurt and stupid that after I gave him my all, he could walk all over me like I was nothing. I felt used and foolish to have believed everything Leon had said to me about how beautiful I was, that he needed me, and how special I was to him. I realized it was all lies that he'd used to take advantage of me and only to get what he wanted. I was naïve and didn't have a clue that I was being manipulated and I didn't see the heartbreak that was lurking right around the corner. At that moment, I believed that I would never experience anything like that again. I knew it would be hard for me to trust anyone again. I felt like there was no reason for me to go on any longer, so I tried to commit suicide.

When I got home, I put my things in my room and went downstairs and took fifteen of what I thought were my mother's small red blood pressure pills. After swallowing them all, I went back to my room and shut my door. I lay on my bed, thinking about all the pain I'd experienced in my life. I was tired of being hurt, mistreated, and misunderstood. I felt like I couldn't take life anymore.

Before long, I felt the urge to vomit and defecate at the same time. I felt a harsh pressure in my stomach, which felt like someone was squeezing my organs. Even walking over to the bathroom was painful. I called out for my mother and told her what I'd done. She was angry, calling me stupid and that I was lucky they were only iron pills. She told me I'd better be glad I hadn't died, then walked away without another word. I don't know why my mother treated me that way, but no matter what, I always loved my mother. I believe my mother behaved that way because of how her mother had treated her. I couldn't stop crying and

Unsure of what to do next, I went back into my room and lay down, praying to God for help. I was at my lowest point, feeling like no one loved me or cared. God was all I had left, so I talked to Him until I fell asleep.

The next morning, I felt much better and the pain in my stomach was gone. I knew there was a God, as I got ready for school and thanked Him for helping me, protecting me, and keeping me alive. I was grateful for the strength He had given me to face another day at school. I walked into the building, feeling much better and determined to leave what happened between Leon and me in the past. But he wasn't planning to make that easy for me. He tried his best to win me back over once he saw I was moving on and not giving him the time of day. The more I shunned him, the more he got the message. It seemed to set in that I didn't have time for his games anymore.

I began playing sports to occupy my time and energy. I also began focusing more on my schoolwork and giving my attention to the right things. Over time, several guys tried to talk to me and, although I talked to a few of them, I was guarded. I never gave any of them my full attention until I reached the 11th grade. My hard work paid off because not only was I was the captain of the cheerleading team, but I was also captain of the female weightlifting team and the president of the key club, which was a leadership club. One day I was helping my team with drills during practice while the boys' basketball team was practicing nearby. I looked up to see a guy running in the hallway and recognized him as a member of the basketball team. He was so handsome that he took my breath away. His smile and straight white teeth stole my attention and I could barely focus. I noticed he was looking my way and smiling at me, so I asked my team who he was. The co-captain, Patti, heard me asking about him and discreetly told her friend to get his phone number for her. Shortly afterward, I began seeing them together often and word around school was they were an item.

Her betrayal hurt so badly, I decided to be done with dealing with females after that. I remained professional and laser-focused on finishing our cheer season successfully. Patti was a senior and I knew I only had to deal with her for a little while more and frankly, she wasn't worth risking blowing everything I'd worked hard to achieve. I learned to keep things to myself and that not everyone who seems to be in your corner is actually rooting for you.

SECTION THREE

SEEKING FAITH

During my senior year, I met with the principal and asked him if I could run for class president. He told me that as long as I met the requirements, it wouldn't be a problem. Once I confirmed that I was qualified to run, I threw my hat in the ring along with two other candidates. I organized my campaign and was voted class president of the class of '09. To go from being in special education classes to winning the most coveted student office position was a huge accomplishment for me. In the history of the school, that had never been done. Many people were not aware that I was enrolled in special education classes because I was also taking traditional classes. I realized that anything is possible and that I could achieve anything I put my mind to doing. My situation or circumstance didn't matter – only the degree of my will and determination. My teachers always told me that I was a unique person that gave my all in every situation. It took a personal commitment to get to know myself and my abilities in order to gain the confidence I needed to pursue great things for myself.

After the breakup with Leon, I was able to clearly see what I was capable of accomplishing. Winning class president from a special education status was an honor that showed me the type of leader I was and what was in store for me. I had some ideas for the senior class, and I was eager to make them happen. While walking down the hallway, Patti's ex-boyfriend, Eugene, bumped into me in the hallway, causing me to drop some papers. He helped me pick them up, apologizing for not paying attention. We locked eyes and I told him that it was okay. We shared a smile before parting ways. I looked back at him a few times and I knew he was sneaking peeks at me as well.

Later that day, I asked a friend of mine to ask him if he had a girlfriend. He told her no and glanced at me watching from down the hall. He smiled, then gave her his phone number to give to me. When my friend returned with the news and his number, I couldn't stop smiling. I couldn't wait to get home and call him. As soon as I got home that afternoon, I went straight to my bedroom and closed the door. The phone rang twice before he answered. I was nervous at first, but we ended up talking for almost two hours. At school the next day, we couldn't stay away from each other. I had three free periods and so did he, so we spent that time getting to know one another better. Talking on the phone had been great, but the face-to-face conversations were much better.

I found myself being painfully honest with Eugene about my past. I told him about my relationship with Leon and how he'd hurt me. I also told him about my suicide attempt. I was nervous about divulging the details, but something in me hoped he would be understanding and compassionate concerning my past. I felt myself growing emotional because I didn't want to experience that type of pain again. He gently grabbed my face while looking into my eyes and told me he would never hurt me. The tears in his eyes and the intensity behind them were convincing and I felt my heart begin to open again. I felt confident that he was the one for me.

Eventually, we made our relationship official and things were going well between us. A little while later, Eugene proposed to me and I said yes. We moved out of our parents' homes and got a place together while still seniors in high school. My mother knew I was responsible enough to live on my own. She saw how happy I was with him and that he was one of the best things that had happened to me. I was over the moon with contentment, in disbelief that I'd found the love of my life. One month after moving into our apartment, I got pregnant. We only had two months left in the school year. I was in a happy place in my life, but I was also afraid. We chose to keep our good news to ourselves until we were ready to inform our families.

I began noticing that we weren't spending our free periods together at school anymore. One day, when I got home, I asked him, "Where have you been going on your free periods at school?" He responded that he was spending that time in the classroom, catching up on his work. It made sense because we were at the end of our senior year and it was crunch time. I figured he was making sure all of his assignments were in to meet his graduating requirements. I didn't question him anymore about it.

One day while I was in the shower, I overheard him on the phone with someone. He was laughing and having a great time. What alerted me that something was wrong was hearing him say, "Girl, you know I…" before he lowered his voice. That red flag was enough to make me break my rule of never going through someone else's phone. I felt like I had no choice at that point. When I turned the water off and got out of the shower, he instantly turned the game back on and ended his call. Yet another red flag that led me to believe that he'd been talking to a female. His suspicious behavior hurt me, and I was confused, racking my brain on what I'd done wrong. I'd always felt like my relationship with Eugene was different than the one with Leon. He'd asked me to marry him, moved in with him, and we had a baby on the way. I didn't understand how he was willing to risk all we had for another female. I stayed in the bathroom for a while, attempting to get myself together and avoid making a decision that I would later regret. I decided to hold off on checking his phone until he had gone to sleep. When I emerged from the bathroom, he looked at me and smiled, asking me how my shower was. I smiled back and told him it was great, and we watched television for a while before he went to sleep. As soon as he dozed off, I grabbed his phone and headed to the bathroom. He had deleted all of his text messages and recent calls, confirming my suspicion that he was hiding something from me. I was baffled at how he could do this to us. I went back into our bedroom and cried myself to sleep.

The next morning, we got ready for school and all the while, I told myself not to react until I found out who she was. I began paying more attention to his daily routine. I approached him in the lunchroom and when he saw me walking up, he tried to slip a piece of paper beneath his notebook. I grabbed the paper and saw that it had a female's script writing on it. He claimed they were notes from a female classmate from a ninth-grade class he had to make up. When I determined which class he was talking about, I walked past the classroom door and found him talking and laughing with a girl instead of paying attention to the teacher. I watched their body language and knew she was the female he'd been dealing with. After the class ended, I waited by the door when he walked out and saw me standing his face looked as if he'd seen a ghost. He had walked out with the girl and I made sure to happily greet him with a "hey, bae". I gave him a hug and she walked away, looking upset.

I told him, "It sure looked like you were having a good ol' time with your friend." Then I walked away. He wasn't a fool, so he figured out that once we got home, we were going to have a serious argument. He called my phone repeatedly, but I didn't answer. Before the end of the day, two friends of mine who were sisters told me that their little sister had been talking to Eugene. They let me know that they'd tried to tell her to stop talking to him because he was in a relationship, but she'd refused. I thanked them for informing me and at the end of the school day, Eugene tried his best to get back on my good side. Despite his best efforts, he failed. When we pulled up to our apartment, he opened the door for me, which he had never done before. I told him to move out of my way and once we entered our apartment, I let him have it. I asked him how could he play me like that and how could he risk all that we had? I asked to see his phone and he fought me tooth and nail. He swore up and down that she was just a friend who was helping him so that he could pass his class. That was when I stepped up in his face and let him know that I'd witnessed their behavior and there was no way they could be platonic. I told him how her own sisters had confirmed the nature of their relationship.

The look on his face gave him away. I snatched his phone from his hand and went into the bathroom, locking the door behind me. He hadn't deleted their last texts and the nature of their conversation was similar to our own. They sent pictures to one another and she let him know that he could do whatever he wanted to her. I was outdone, hurt, and devastated. I came out of the bathroom and asked him to call her and end whatever they had going on. He tried to protest, but the look on my face let him know that I was not taking no for an answer. When he called her on speakerphone, she picked up right away.

He said, "I can't talk to you anymore. I have a girlfriend."

She simply laughed, said okay, and hung up. When he looked up at me, he had tears in his eyes and began apologizing profusely, claiming to never have meant to hurt me. He didn't know what he was thinking.

I told him, "You hurt me. Something you said you'd never do." When I walked away, he grabbed me and continued to plead for my forgiveness. I said, "I spilled my heart out to you and you walked over it like I was nothing. I don't think I can ever trust you again."

READY TO LET GO

I knew I had some thinking to do to make sure I'd made the right decision for my unborn child. I didn't want my baby to also grow up without knowing their father. I really loved Eugene and I wanted things to work out between us. I decided to stick around and try to make things work with him. When I saw the girl the next day at school, I asked her if I could speak to her. When she agreed, I let her know that I wasn't upset with her, but I was letting her know that Eugene and I were engaged and expecting. She said she hadn't known he had a girlfriend and that he hadn't said anything about me or our unborn child. She said he was acting single and that she'd even been to our apartment a few times and they'd made out while she was there. She said her sisters had warned her that he had a girlfriend, but she hadn't believed them because he'd never acted like he was in a relationship.

Hearing her words infuriated me and I accused her of lying. She responded that she didn't have a reason to lie and began describing our bedroom and some of the items I had in my bathroom. When she let me know she'd been in the apartment, I told her I would ask Eugene about it. She said she'd felt bad because she hadn't known about me while dealing with him. A part of me didn't want to believe her, but I knew I couldn't argue with the facts. She'd known things she couldn't have known if she hadn't been to our apartment. I left her and went to find Eugene. When I did, I slapped him and said words that only a hurt soul would say.

I asked him, "You took her to our apartment and had sex with her in our bed?"

He didn't say a word to defend himself; he just walked away embarrassed. At the end of the day, I took the bus to my parents' house. I didn't want to go back to the apartment and deal with him. He blew up my phone and I refused to accept his calls. Once I arrived at my parents' home, my mother asked me what was wrong. I let her know that Eugene had been cheating on me but didn't mention the pregnancy. She called him and asked him to come to her house. When he arrived, my mother asked him if he'd cheated on me. He denied it, stating he'd only touched her butt.

Although I knew my mother hadn't believed him, she told Eugene, "Okay, so that means you cheated. You can't do things like that with other females while in a committed relationship." Even though I was ready to end things with him right then and there, my parents talked to us, letting us know that relationships are hard, and that forgiveness is the key to working things out. Unbeknownst to them, our unborn child was the only reason I'd even considered seeing things through with Eugene at that point. While I appreciated everything, my parents had to say, they were unaware of how much I'd confided in Eugene about what I'd gone through in my past and the toll it had taken on me. I was sure he'd known right from wrong and still hadn't cared about how his actions affected me, so I figured why should I?

He eventually stopped talking to the girl and apologized for messing around with her, although he'd never admitted to having sex with her. I had never been able to accept his apology because I didn't believe it was sincere. A week later, when we'd graduated from high school, I found out he'd been talking to another girl whom he'd met while playing basketball at the rec center. My first instinct was to meet up with the girl and try to fight her, but I thought about the fact that I was pregnant and didn't need to be fighting anyone. It was at that point that I decided to hold Eugene accountable for his actions. The small amount of trust I had in him was gone at that point.

SECTION FIVE

RISING ABOVE ALL THINGS

I made up my mind to work and save up enough money to leave him. I had my choice of accepting a city job or one of two good construction jobs. But leaving was easier said than done. My fear of raising a child alone was stifling. I began hoping for a miracle instead and began working at the city job with great benefits and stability. At first, the job seemed to be going well, but over time, I began noticing the unprofessional behavior. During a pole climbing class at work, I was one of the only females who could make it to the top and I also learned everything they taught us quickly.

One day, I fainted while at the top of the pole and, if it weren't for the harness, I would have fallen off of it. Once I was taken to the hospital and they ran some tests, they discovered I was dehydrated and pregnant. When word got out at work that I was pregnant, they put me on administrative work only. Isabella came during a winter storm at Huron Hospital. Although I'd helped raise my siblings, I hadn't experienced pregnancy before. The moment I looked into her eyes, I pledged to be the best mother I could be to her and that she would never experience the things I had during my childhood. I vowed not to use drugs, make her feel unwanted, and or to ever treat her any different from her future siblings. She was my precious jewel and I held her close to me, cherishing her and showering her with love. Some people thought I was overprotective, but I wanted to give her the world.

After my maternity leave, they barely wanted to allow me to return to work. I was told that I'd have to complete the pole climbing class I'd previously been removed from. I understood and was fine with that. When I resumed the class, I was back on the pole and something else happened. I felt something wet and warm trickling down my legs. I wasn't feeling any pain at the time, but later found out I was hemorrhaging and had severely ripped my abdominal muscles. The doctor confirmed that I had been putting too much strain on my body too quickly after having the baby. I was in unbearable pain and had to take a leave from work for another three weeks. When I returned, they put me back on administrative work until the commercial driver's license classes began. I'd previously earned my Commercial Driver's License (CDL) temps, but a Class A license was needed for my role in order to become a truck driver for the company. This was a better fit for me because pole climbing was very hard on my body after I had my baby. The Class A trucks were no joke and I initially doubted my ability to pass the maneuverability portion of the exam. As it turned out, I was able to pass the Pre-Trip portion of the exam, which is a test that covered my knowledge of internal and external inspection. But I failed the maneuverability portion. I was upset and felt discouraged, but my dad told me to never give up and to try again. I reattempted the test, trying to remain positive, but I knew that if I didn't pass it, I wouldn't earn my CDL and would lose my job. My temporary license expired in the meantime, so I faced my fears and earned my temps again, retook the Class A exam, and passed it all. Finally, able to get my Class A CDL, I was overjoyed and believed that I would be hired for a full-time position. But that never happened to me.

I was devastated and would confide in Eugene about my concerns and uncertainty about my situation. I would share my thoughts about possibly starting to look for another job and he would tell me that I needed to make up my mind on what I wanted to do. I felt like he didn't care about my happiness or what I wanted to do in life. What made it even harder was he wasn't able to keep a stable job at the time. If he didn't care for the job, he would quit without having another one lined up. I felt that it was unfair for him to think it was okay sticking me with paying all of the bills while he was at home, playing video games. I needed more help from him than keeping our daughter while I was at work. After a while, my uncle talked him into joining the military and Eugene joined the National Guard. Those who were married made more money to help provide for their family, so he brought up the idea of us getting married. I told him that I loved him, but that I wasn't in love with him anymore and I also did not trust him. He told me I would learn to love and trust him again. Although I disagreed with his stance, I knew that we needed more income, so I decided to do what I needed to do for our family.

We got married at his family's church shortly after. A part of me hoped that taking those vows would help us strengthen our relationship and begin moving in the right direction. Clearly, I did not know anything about marriage. To be honest, I was at my wit's end at that time and didn't know what else to do. When he joined the military, he began a ten-week basic training and I hoped that our time apart would help us get a clearer perspective on the relationship. I focused my time and efforts on restarting a youth outreach entertainment group I'd started in high school called The Beauties. I was their manager and choreographer and I wrote all of their songs. I'd initially included my sisters, Essence and Autumn, and our god sister. I'd designed it to keep them out of trouble. The core values were leadership, tenacity, persistence, and learning the value of hard work. They were invited to perform at schools, recreation centers, amusement parks, and festivals. They'd even won a few dance competitions. I loved seeing the joy on their faces when they won their competitions and earned praise for their performances. In creating this group, I gave young girls the camaraderie, love, and support I'd never had. They could take and use this experience with them for a lifetime. They were music artists with published songs to share with their children one day. One of my favorite songs I'd written for them was "Bullying". The message was positive and passionate and one that I related to. It was easy to write and came from my heart. It's available on YouTube.

I was curious to learn how us spending time apart would feel and I was grateful that I'd actually begun missing him. We wrote letters to one another, expressing how much we missed one another. When he returned home, we were in a good place. It felt like our relationship was finally getting back on track. In the meantime, my girls had lost interest in performing. Eugene didn't like all of the time I'd been spending while working with The Beauties and thought it was a waste of my time. He refused to come out and support our shows. Things began to worsen, and he signed up for overseas duty without telling me. I tried to talk him out of it and asked him to go with me to speak to the pastor, but he refused. I gave up. By then, we had a son together and I would have hoped that having two small children would have inspired him to find a good job and stay at home with his family. But he was still determined to go overseas.

So, I was a single mother of two children having to do everything on my own. It was hard at first, but I got used to doing what I needed to do for myself and my babies over time. I did whatever I needed to do to provide for them. Even though we had a joint bank account and I had the money I needed for his half of the bills it did not make up for him being absent in our home. When he left, it showed me that I didn't want a man in my life who only thought of himself when making critical life decisions. To add insult to injury, I later found out that he was still talking to other women while we were married. That taught me a life lesson: having a child with a man will not keep him. Although I was afraid to let him go, I gave up on our relationship.

He was gone for four months when I began talking to a guy named Curtis that I used to go to high school with. He started liking my posts on Instagram and I recognized him right away. He was a senior while I was a freshman and I'd always thought he was handsome. I'd had a crush on him, but he was popular, so I never thought he noticed me or that I had a chance of getting with him. On Instagram, he'd commented on one of my posts that he wanted me to be his manager. He said he loved to write poetry and wanted to do something with it. I direct messaged him because I loved expressing myself through poetry and songwriting. I asked him if he remembered me. At first, he said he didn't, but as I began to mention other things about our experience there, he said he remembered me and that I was in a relationship at the time that he knew me. Curtis told me that Leon, my so-called first love, had been messing around with his girlfriend while Leon and I were together, which was news to me. After messaging each other for a while, we decided to exchange phone numbers and began talking on the phone. We found out that we had a lot in common: where we lived, the people we knew, our mothers having the same birthdays, and some other uncanny coincidences. We would talk every day until we grew tired, knowing we had to go to work in the morning. But I didn't want our conversation to end. When we would hang up, I couldn't stop smiling and would go to bed happy. I would text him as soon as I woke up, eager to talk to him and anticipating the great conversations we would have.

After a few months, I felt comfortable enough to share details about my marriage with Curtis. He was not only empathetic to my situation; he would offer great advice on how we could focus on each other to save our marriage. He was a great friend and I believed I could speak to him about anything. He came to my youth group's shows and video shoots and supported everything I did. When my husband returned from overseas, I tried to use Curtis' advice and made a sincere effort to save our relationship. It seemed like the harder I tried, the more he resisted and pulled away from me. Nothing seemed to work, and it seemed like all he'd wanted was to leave our marriage.

A few months after his return, the house was a mess and he never wanted to help with the kids or with any of the household responsibilities. I would go to work all day and when I came home, he would be exactly where I'd left him. He was lazy and all that seemed to hold his attention were his video games. As soon as the kids and I got settled in, he would jump up, saying he was going to work out or play basketball. I would tell him that he needed to get a job and stop lying around the house and he would get mad and leave, staying out until all times of the night. After he left, I would call Curtis and tell him I was ready to give up because none of my efforts seemed to work. There wasn't any connection between us anymore and he'd refused to seek help with me. I'd suggested going to see our pastor or to see a counselor, because, despite his infidelity, I still wanted to make things work between us because of our children.

Curtis would always listen and tell me positive things to keep me in the right frame of mind. He would ensure me that everything would be okay, and I believed him. I continued to try to make my marriage work until he gave me a reason not to. One day, he left without signing out of his Facebook account on our computer. When I looked in his messenger, I saw that he'd been having inappropriate conversations with a female from the job he'd just started. That was it for me. I knew we just weren't meant to be together and I refused to continue to have my needs thrown on the back burner while he continued to do him as if he didn't have a wife and kids at home.

I had a serious talk with Eugene the first chance I got. I told him that I believed it would be best if we went our separate ways because I was very unhappy, we didn't communicate with one another, and we didn't have anything in common anymore. The other women, the lies, and the refusal to accept responsibility for his actions were all wearing me down. I let him know things between us had to end now.

His initial response was, "Okay. I'll sign the papers, but it's going to be hard for you to find someone else. No man wants a woman with two kids." Then he laughed. I let him know he'd be surprised what a man wants, but I wasn't looking for a man, I was looking for him to leave. I knew that if God wanted me to have a man, He would send the right one my way. He said I would be a miserable person once the children grow up and leave the house. I just smiled at him without saying a word. I decided it was time to show and prove. When those papers arrived in the mail a few weeks later, that smug look on his face was gone.

He asked, "So you're really serious about getting a divorce?" I told him it was time for me to live my life and focus my time and energy on raising two happy children. At first, he acted like he was upset, but shortly after he saw that I was serious about leaving him, random women began popping up. We had a few more months left in our lease and he was sleeping upstairs while the children and I slept downstairs. Curtis and I began going out together to bars, restaurants, and to the movies. He too had just ended a difficult relationship and he was single and enjoying his life at the time. He didn't have any children and it was hard to believe that a woman let a good man like him slip away. He always treated me with respect and kindness. He opened doors, provided a listening ear, and was supportive whenever I needed him.

After getting the run around from my job at the city, I began thinking about how hard it would be to try to support myself and two children while earning ten dollars an hour. I still had a Class-A CDL, so I began looking for jobs at other places. Soon after, I received a call about a transportation opportunity. I successfully completed the interview and was pleased to be moving forward in the process. In the meantime, the city job reached out and informed me that I would have to take a retake a test in order to keep my job. Although I'd already passed it, they insisted that I take it immediately. I failed it by four points. They terminated me and I was devastated they played me like that. I couldn't stop crying, frustrated with their constant unfair treatment of me. I began feeling discouraged, but I told myself to keep the faith that God would make a way for me. I remembered that I had another job waiting for me. They called with a job offer, so once one door closed, another one opened.

STILL I RISE

Curtis was by my side every step of the way. He always believed in my ability to succeed and supported everything that I did. I began developing feelings for him and wondered if he was the man God had been preparing me for. He was everything I needed in a man. I think he began to realize that I was vetting him because I asked him if he was talking to any females. After the divorce was final, I felt a weight lift from my shoulders, and it felt good to finally be free from an unhealthy, emotionally draining marriage. I had a talk with Eugene, letting him know that I would never keep the children away from him, but he would have to make sure he continued to be a full-time father.

At first, everything went smoothly. Eugene did his part and was active with the children. But once he realized I had a male friend in my life, jealousy took over. He told me he didn't want another man around his children. I let him know that Curtis would be respectful of him and that he wanted to meet him before coming around the children. Eugene asked how long I'd been friends with Curtis, and I let him know we'd known each other for a while. He began accusing me of cheating on him and although I told him I'd never cheated on him. I mentioned how Curtis had always given me advice on how to work on our marriage when we were having our issues, but of course, he didn't believe me. He asked me if I liked Curtis and I told him he was a great guy and that I did. I was surprised when Eugene agreed to meet him. I was pleased that he was willing to meet the man who would be around his children because he had his funny acting days.

When I informed Curtis, that Eugene was ready to meet him, I didn't hold back on letting him know how I felt about him. I told him I believed that God had sent him to me. He smiled, showing his nice teeth and dimples and replied, "You deserve better. You're a great woman and any man would be lucky to have you." I looked him in the eyes and told him I hoped that man would be him. He just smiled. He met Eugene and shortly after, we began dating. When he finally met my children, they loved him. Once Curtis began coming around more, Eugene began to slack off on his fatherly duties. He would be late picking the kids up and eventually stopped getting them altogether, always armed with an excuse. One day, he left my son at daycare while I was at work and wasn't allowed to get off to pick him up. I was so grateful that Curtis was able to step in for me. It hadn't been the first time Eugene had done that. He'd also left my children alone at his house to run errands before and would leave them in the car unattended. I tried my best to work with him, but he made it difficult for me.

I often worked weekends, so Curtis would cancel his plans to watch the kids for me each weekend, dropping me off and picking me up from work. He proved his reliability to me time and time again and was there for me when I needed him the most. I fell in love with him because he was everything I'd ever wanted in a man. I often felt like I was dreaming when it came to him because he seemed too good to be true. Eventually, we moved in together and things between me and Eugene grew worse. He didn't want the children living with Curtis and did everything in his power to disrupt our relationship. He tried to convince me to resume our relationship and I let him know that wasn't going to happen. I was happy with Curtis and wasn't planning on looking back. I told him to put all of that energy into focusing on his children. Shortly after, Eugene moved down the street from us and became active in the children's lives again. Then he announced he had a girlfriend. I was happy for him, but I requested to meet her since she was going to be around my children. Eugene refused to introduce us, stating that it wasn't necessary. I left it

alone and continued to let him see the kids, which would be whenever it was convenient for him.

We wouldn't see eye to eye on his erratic schedule with seeing the children, but Curtis stayed out of it. But Eugene's girlfriend didn't give me the same courtesy. She texted me from his phone, then delete the message so he wouldn't see it. Whenever I would question him about the texts, he wouldn't know what I was referring to. I let him know that his girlfriend was contacting me from his phone, and he denied it, stating she wasn't like that. I was fed up, so I looked her up on Facebook and messaged her directly. I was respectful but her replies were combative, so we didn't see eye to eye either. We didn't like one another and Eugene informed me that she was threatened because I was his first wife and had his first child. I could see at that point how immature she was and that she couldn't get over the fact that Eugene had a life before her. Over time, I started to realize that Eugene liked the fact that she and I would get into it. He never attempted to step in and diffuse things between us. Once Curtis attempted to intervene, Eugene finally began to mediate the situation. I let Eugene know that he'd have to come alone when picking up and dropping off the kids. She was far too disrespectful to me to come to my home and I refused to go back to my former violent ways.

Eugene tried to convince me that it wasn't that serious, but on the other hand, he would tell me things about his girlfriend and tell her things about me. I realized at that point that he wanted to fuel the drama between us. I told him he had a lot of growing up to do and I stopped talking to him altogether about anything that didn't pertain to our children. I would shut him down when he tried to bring anything else to me. Things instantly improved for me and I was able to focus on my household. We were later pleased to find out that we were expecting our first child together. When Eugene found out, the madness restarted, and he was dead set on destroying our happiness. Anytime he heard about anything good happening in my life, he would begin treating our children differently. He would complain about having to buy them things, arguing that child support should handle his half of the expense, but he barely paid child support. Eventually, I stopped asking him for money for the children because Curtis would step up and help take care of their needs. As Curtis and I became more serious, it became clear that he was the one God had sent for me.

After a year of us living together, I gave birth to our beautiful daughter. I felt blessed to be able to give him his first child. When she was just a few weeks old, Curtis asked me to marry him on bended knee on Christmas day. He'd already asked for my parents' blessing. I emphatically accepted the proposal from the man of my dreams. I was honored to call him my fiancé and was in disbelief that I was actually about to plan a wedding with this amazing man. My heart had been broken many times before and, for a long time, I didn't believe that real love would happen for me. Every time I thought it was real, something would always disrupt things. But I knew this time would be different because it felt different. The level of passionate love Curtis had for me had surpassed all of the others I'd experienced in relationships before him. I felt his love deep down in my soul. We had so many common experiences and coincidences in our lives and knew a lot of the same people while growing up. The fact that both of our parents' birthdays were so close, it felt like we were meant to be soulmates.

Our wedding day was one of the best days of my life. I became the beautiful princess I'd always wanted to be. I looked and felt like royalty and the day was dedicated to me. It meant so much to me because my prom and graduation had been ruined by my sister intentionally. Growing up, my parents would always make me apologize to her when we would get into it when it would mostly be a result of her picking on me, calling me names, and making me feel like I was nothing. When she wasn't doing those things, she was completely ignoring and disowning me while at school because I was in special education classes. I felt like I had no one to look up to while younger and made an effort to ensure my little sisters didn't have the same experience. So, I decided not to invite her to my wedding day because that day wasn't going to be about her and her drama. I told her I would always love her, but I couldn't share my special day with her. She told me she hadn't planned on attending anyway. I told her that I wanted the resolve the bad blood between us but she didn't have anything positive to say, so I told her

God bless you and wished her the best. I knew my parents would be upset about it, but they would just have to understand. It turned out to be the best decision I'd ever made. I knew it was time for me to live my life and have been able to focus on loving myself more than ever since then.

Curtis has also helped me realize my self-worth by urging me to let go of all of the negative people in my life. I've been able to accomplish several personal goals by realizing that lacking an ideal past doesn't mean you can't grow and strive to manifest better things in your life. We all have the opportunity to become anything we want and to make the best of our situations. Yes, life will be hard, but consistency allows you to realize your dreams. I am a living testimony of that. I have been molested, lied to, bullied, ridiculed, and unwanted. I have been at my lowest point and have felt like I had no one to talk to. I've attempted to take my own life. But, through it all, I have remained prayerful – even when I felt like my problems were beyond the power of prayer. Then, one day, my prayers were answered. The first answer was when the drug use in my household ceased. That's when I realized that prayer worked. I learned to keep trying, to never give up, and hold my head high on my worst day while holding on to the faith that change will come.

Today, I am 30 years old and happily married to the love of my life. I have four beautiful children. I own a beauty supply store and will be expanding it soon. It pays to turn negative situations and turn them into positive opportunities. That has been my formula for success. I refuse to let anyone tell me what I'm incapable of and believe that I'm capable of doing anything I put my mind to and that is all the empowerment I need. My life is a testimony of that. After experiencing life's trials and tribulations, I know it's okay to start over. You can reset your mind with positive affirmations. Tell yourself, "I am beautiful, I am smart, I am me." Once you plant those seeds in your mind, you will grow to love yourself even more. Everything you do starts with your mindset. If you continue working on yourself and build yourself up, you will become successful.

On the following pages, I have provided some space for journaling. I would like you to take the opportunity to encourage yourself with the powerful words below. Say them daily and watch how they change your mindset and your self-reflection. Release all of the toxic thoughts and begin to let the good energy come in. Repeat these words aloud and rewrite them on the following pages: I AM BEAUTIFUL, I AM SMART, I AM ME… I forgive and release myself from everything in my past.

Now watch yourself flourish. We have to break the generational curses in our lives and plant positive seeds into one another.

That's the only way we can build an unstoppable army of greatness.

Sincerely,
Beauty Turned Beast

SECTION SEVEN

EMBRACE YOUR JOURNEY

Remember to look into the mirror each day and say,

"I AM BEAUTIFUL, I AM SMART, I AM ME."

Positive thoughts breed positive energy, so focus your mindset on things that will manifest great things in your life. From there you will notice a substantial shift in your life.

_____

_____

_____

_____

_____

_____

_____

_____

CPSIA information can be obtained
at www.ICGtesting.com
Printed in the USA
LVHW051716271020
669964LV00003B/784

9 781489 729941